# EVERYTHING
# WORLD WAR I

NATIONAL
GEOGRAPHIC
KiDS

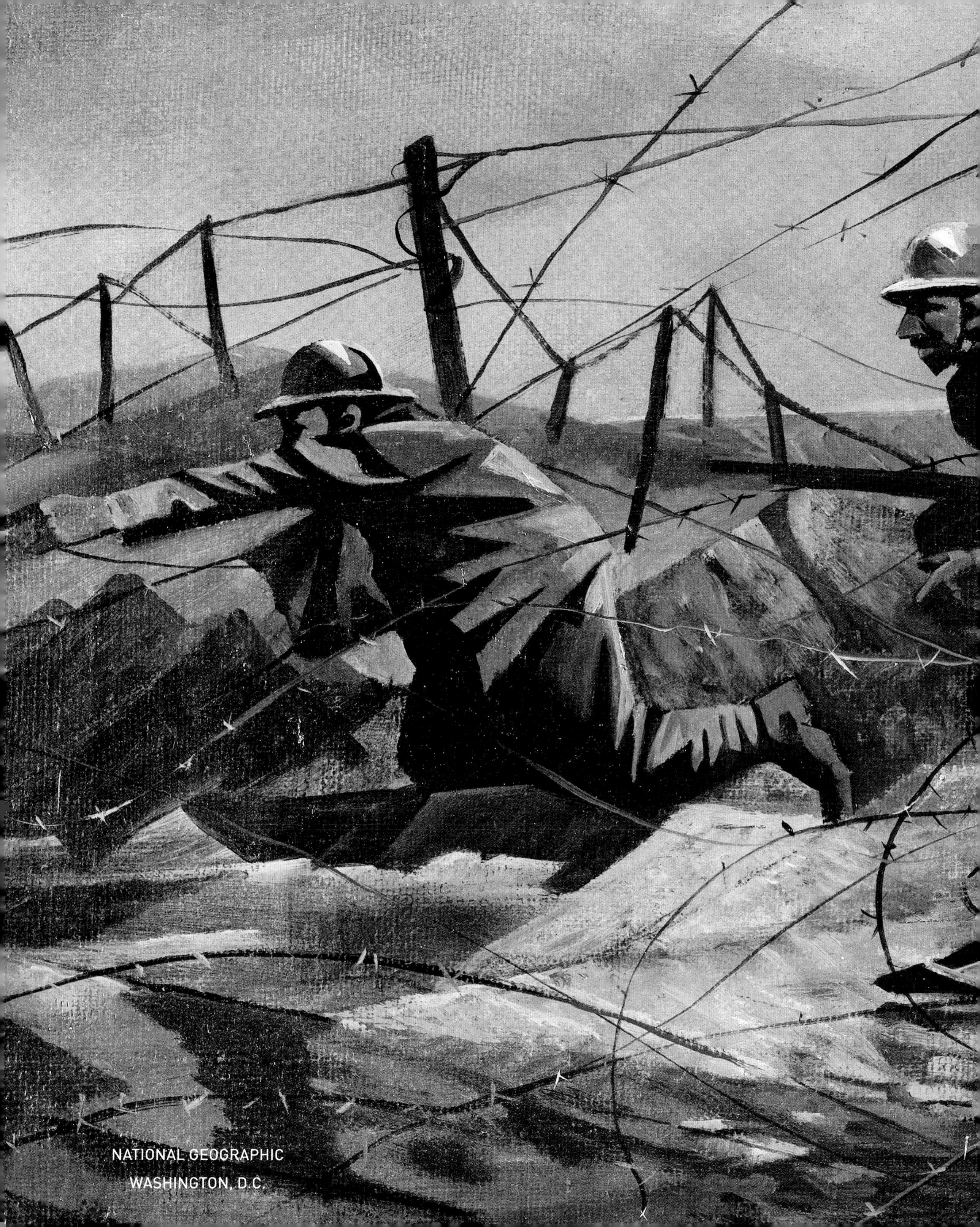

NATIONAL GEOGRAPHIC
WASHINGTON, D.C.

NATIONAL GEOGRAPHIC KiDS

# EVERYTHING WORLD WAR I

BY KAREN LATCHANA KENNEY

With Historian EDWARD G. LENGEL

# CONTENTS

A company of Canadian soldiers leaves a muddy trench on the western front to engage the enemy on the battlefield.

World War I American soldiers, called dough-boys, carry sacks of hand grenades to the front. They keep their heads and bodies low so they won't be shot by enemy snipers.

# INTRODUCTION

## THEY HOPED IT WOULD

**BE A WAR TO END ALL WARS—ONE THAT** would last just months and take few lives. But it ended more than four years later—a muddy and bloody mess that claimed the lives of more than 16 million people.

The First World War (1914–1918), was the world's first modern war. Weapons such as heavy artillery, poison gas, tanks, battleships, and aircraft made this a war like no other.

Millions of men and women served their countries during World War I, also known as the Great War. Soldiers fought on land, on the sea, and in the air. Whole societies supported the war effort. This was a total war, and everyone was involved.

Soldiers fought from muddy trenches that stretched along the front lines, and battles lasted from days to months. The Great War changed the world forever. Ready to learn how? It's time to find out EVERYTHING about World War I.

## EXPLORER'S CORNER

### Hi! I'm Ed Lengel.

I spend most of my time learning and writing about military history, especially World War I. To be a military historian, you need to understand how armies work and what happens in battles. That means learning about the history of wars from ancient times—when Greeks, Persians, Romans, and others were duking it out—to the present day. I also think it's important to visit battlefields and listen to veterans so that they can explain what war means to them. I learn about World War I by reading soldiers' diaries and letters. Then I walk the battlefields, which are still covered with craters, trenches, abandoned equipment, and even unexploded bombs. Come walk the battlefields with me as we learn about one of the most interesting and tragic wars in history. Watch your step!

World War I was known for its trench warfare, where ditches about seven feet (2 m) deep were dug to position troops on the front lines. Storming an enemy trench was dangerous, as it required soldiers to leave their own trench and cross no-man's-land while under enemy fire.

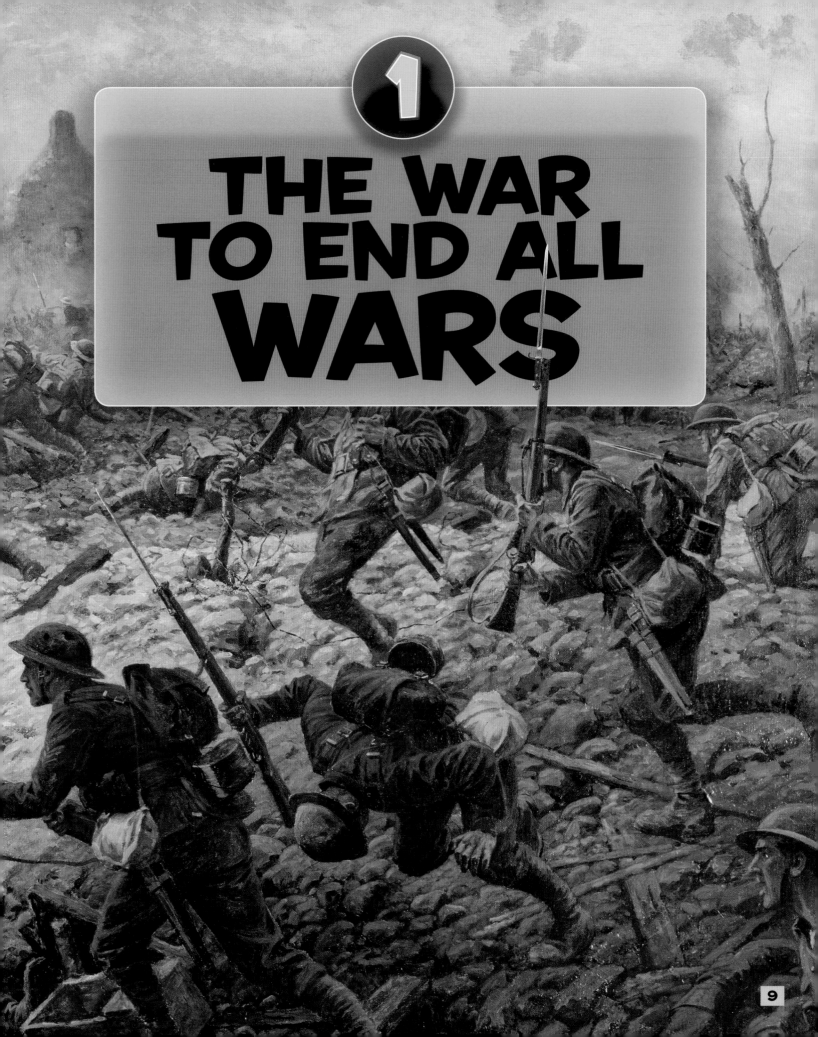

# THE WAR TO END ALL WARS

# WHAT WAS WORLD WAR I?

## WORLD WAR I WAS THE WORLD'S FIRST MAJOR INTERNATIONAL WAR. IT'S ALSO A WAR THAT HAD MANY CAUSES—ALL OF THEM

rooted in how the world was run 100 years ago. In the early 1900s, Europe's dominant powers were empires, or groups of countries and territories under one ruler. These empires made alliances with other empires to protect each other during war. When one declared war, as the Austro-Hungarian Empire did against Serbia in 1914, their allies followed them.

### HOW AND WHY: THE ASSASSINATION OF AN ARCHDUKE

The immediate cause of the war was the assassination of the heir to the Austro-Hungarian throne, Archduke Franz Ferdinand, on June 28, 1914. Years earlier, in 1908, Austria-Hungary forcibly made the territory of Bosnia-Herzegovina part of its empire, angering the people living there. After the archduke was assassinated in Sarajevo, Bosnia, by a Bosnian Serb, Austria-Hungary declared war on Serbia. Austria-Hungary's ally Germany supported the empire. Serbia was supported by its ally Russia, which was in turn supported by its ally, France. When Germany attacked France and Belgium, the United Kingdom joined the war against Germany. The war soon spread from there.

Archduke Franz Ferdinand and his wife, Sophie, just before they were assassinated.

## WWI AT A GLANCE

**JUNE 28, 1914**
- Serbian Gavrilo Princip assassinates Archduke Franz Ferdinand of Austria-Hungary.

**JULY 28, 1914**
- Austria-Hungary declares war against Serbia.

**JULY 31, 1914**
- Russia, Serbia's ally, mobilizes its armed forces.

**AUGUST 1–4, 1914**
- Germany joins with Austria-Hungary and declares war on Russia, Belgium, and France.

# FRONTLINE FIGHTING

Front lines in war are the areas where armies meet and engage in battle. In World War I, there were two main "fronts"—the western front and the eastern front. The western front cut across Belgium and France in western Europe. The eastern front was a longer front that stretched throughout eastern Europe from the Baltic Sea in the north to the Black Sea in the south. Other battles took place throughout the world at sea or in German, French, or British colonies in Asia and Africa.

# THE TRIPLE ENTENTE AND THE TRIPLE ALLIANCE

World War I was a war of alliances made by European empires. The opponents came from two groups with names that sound like superhero teams: the Triple Entente and the Triple Alliance. Each of these had three main members but by the end of the war, more than 100 countries had joined the conflict. Some troops came from as far away as New Zealand and Japan. The two main European alliances were:

### THE TRIPLE ENTENTE (OR ALLIES)

- Britain (and its colonies and members of the empire)
- France
- Russia
- Other, smaller countries, and later the United States

### THE TRIPLE ALLIANCE (OR CENTRAL POWERS)

- Germany
- Ottoman Empire
- Austria-Hungary
- And other, smaller countries

**Bulldogs against dachshunds? The Allies and Central Powers are represented as dogs in military dress in this postcard from early in the war. The United States at this time was neutral and is represented by a American terrier with a flag scarf.**

---

**AUGUST 4, 1914**
- Britain declares war against Germany. Canada, Australia, and New Zealand automatically follow Britain into war.

**APRIL 6, 1917**
- The United States enters the war.

**OCTOBER 30, 1918**
- The Ottoman Empire, an ally of Austria-Hungary, withdraws from the war.

**MARCH 3, 1918**
- Russia signs an armistice with Germany and leaves the war.

**NOVEMBER 11, 1918**
- The war ends when Germany and the Allies sign an armistice.

# RALLYING FOR WAR

Posters encouraged men to sign up for service.

## EVERYBODY THOUGHT THE

**WAR WOULD BE OVER QUICKLY. "HOME BY CHRISTMAS"** was what many men who signed up for service told their loved ones. They had no idea how long the war would actually last. Troops were rushed to the front lines from around the world, but most were not prepared for years of brutal warfare.

EVEN A DOG ENLISTS WHY NOT YOU?

**660** MARKET ST. SAN FRANCISCO Or any U.S. Army Recruiting Station

GALLOWAY LITHO. CO. S.F.

## SETTING OUT

Once war was declared, countries had to mobilize, or prepare their troops for war. Some armies, such as Germany's, were larger and more organized prior to the war, while other troops such as the Australian and New Zealand Army Corps (ANZAC), were formed specifically to fight in the Great War. Mobilizing troops took time and money as soldiers had to be trained and transported to the front lines.

**FRONTLINE FACT** ABOUT 1.7 MILLION RUSSIAN SOLDIERS WERE KILLED IN WWI.

# DRAFTING SOLDIERS

What do you do when you have a war to fight and not enough soldiers to fight it? You make civilians join your army! The front lines were deadly places and with soldiers dying every day and not enough volunteers to replace them, countries drafted or conscripted new soldiers. Men were required to enlist for the military and then were randomly chosen to serve during the war. In the United States, men between the ages of 21 and 30 had to register for military service. Nearly 24 million American men signed up and 2.8 million were drafted and served in the war.

The first draft of a U.S. soldier (right) and the attestation papers of a Canadian soldier (below) that show he was drafted and agreed to serve.

## OBJECTING TO WAR

Although many men felt a patriotic duty to sign up as soldiers, some had deep objections or religious beliefs opposed to violence and war and chose not to fight. These men were called conscientious objectors, or COs. Most COs were ridiculed, called cowards, and harassed for their beliefs. Very few were excused from service. They were drafted anyway or thrown in jail if they refused. Some served as noncombatant stretcher bearers and kitchen helpers.

---

3   M. D.   Depot Battalion,   Regtl. No. 3320578
2nd ... BATTALION,
Eastern Ontario Regiment

## PARTICULARS OF RECRUIT
ORIGINAL

DRAFTED UNDER MILITARY SERVICE ACT, 1917

(Class .......... 1 .......... )

1. Surname ............ Rodger

2. Christian name ............ Thomas Kitchem

3. Present address ............ 477 Prince Albert Av. Westmount Montreal

4. Military Service Act letter and number ............

5. Date of birth ............ May 28th 1885

6. Place of birth (town, township or county and country) ............ Montreal P.Q.

7. Married, widower or single ............ Single

8. Religion ............ Presbyterian

9. Trade or calling ............ Telephone & telegraph Engineer

10. Name of next-of-kin ............ Mr T.Rodger

11. Relationship of next-of-kin ............ Father

12. Address of next-of-kin ............ 477 Prince Albert Av Westmount Montreal

13. Whether at present a member of the Active Militia ............ No

14. Particulars of previous military or naval service, if any ............ Nil

15. Medical Examination under Military Service Act:— ............ Jan 24th 1918 Category ............ A 11
   (a) Place ............ Ottawa   (b) Date ............

### DECLARATION OF RECRUIT

I, ............ Thomas Kitchen Rodger ............ , do solemnly declare that the above particulars refer to me, and are true.

*Thos K Rodger* (Signature of Recruit)

### DESCRIPTION ON CALLING UP

|  |  |  | Distinctive marks, and marks indicating congential peculiarities or previous disease. |
|---|---|---|---|
| Apparent age ........ | 32 yrs ........ | 9 mths. | |
| Height ........ | 5 ft ........ | 6½ ins. | |
| Chest measurement { fully expanded ........ | 35 ........ | ins. | N I L |
| range of expansion ........ | 2⅔ ........ | ins. | |
| Complexion ........ | Fair | | |
| Eyes ........ | Blue | | |
| ........ | Light Brown | | |

---

# Boots on the Ground

## 12,000,000
Russian soldiers were mobilized in World War I.

## 11,000,000
German soldiers signed up for service in World War I.

## 8,904,467
British Empire troops served in the war, including soldiers from Canada, Australia, and New Zealand.

## 8,410,000
French and French colony soldiers served in World War I.

## 7,800,000
Austro-Hungarian soldiers served in World War I.

# WHERE IN THE WORLD?

## GLOBAL POWERS

### JOINED FORCES ON THE

battlefields of Europe. From far and near, supplies and troops were sent. Never before had the world seen a war of this size.

## EXPLORER'S CORNER

World War I changed the world. Nobody could escape its effects. Soldiers weren't the only ones whose lives were changed. Around the world, everyone—farmers, factory workers, housewives, and children—had to deal with things such as battles, food shortages, and cultural and political changes. These experiences altered the way people thought about each other and about the world.

### CANADA

As a commonwealth of Great Britain, Canada entered the war automatically with Britain on August 4, 1914. By the end of the war, Canada had sent 619,000 soldiers off to battle. The war helped shape the country's identity in the century that followed.

### UNITED STATES

Most Americans did not want to enter a war thousands of miles away. The country sent artillery and supplies to the Allies, but remained neutral for much of the war, before joining on April 6, 1917.

## ALLIES AND CENTRAL POWERS IN WORLD WAR I

CANADA

UNITED STATES

HAITI

CUBA

HONDURAS

GUATEMALA
NICARAGUA
COSTA RICA

PANAMA

BRITISH GUIANA

FRENCH GUIANA

BRAZIL

The National War Memorial in Ottawa shows Canadian soldiers marching to World War I.

A U.S. recruitment poster encouraged men to join the army after the United States declared war in 1917.

I WANT YOU FOR U.S. ARMY
NEAREST RECRUITING STATION

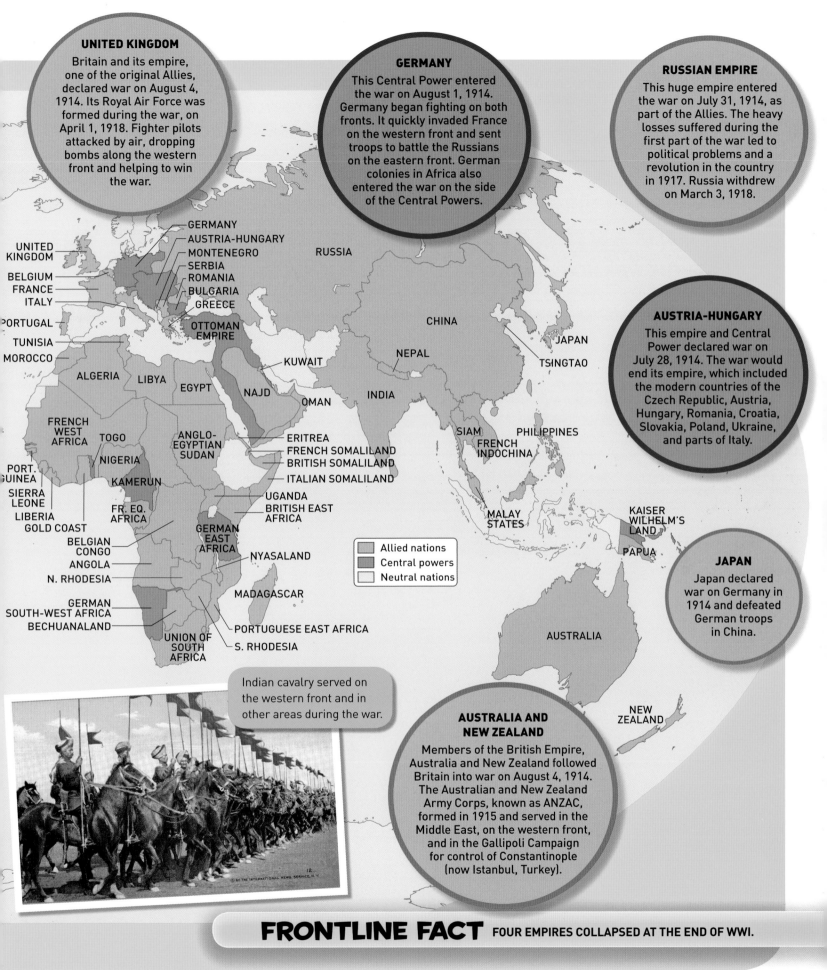

## UNITED KINGDOM

Britain and its empire, one of the original Allies, declared war on August 4, 1914. Its Royal Air Force was formed during the war, on April 1, 1918. Fighter pilots attacked by air, dropping bombs along the western front and helping to win the war.

## GERMANY

This Central Power entered the war on August 1, 1914. Germany began fighting on both fronts. It quickly invaded France on the western front and sent troops to battle the Russians on the eastern front. German colonies in Africa also entered the war on the side of the Central Powers.

## RUSSIAN EMPIRE

This huge empire entered the war on July 31, 1914, as part of the Allies. The heavy losses suffered during the first part of the war led to political problems and a revolution in the country in 1917. Russia withdrew on March 3, 1918.

## AUSTRIA-HUNGARY

This empire and Central Power declared war on July 28, 1914. The war would end its empire, which included the modern countries of the Czech Republic, Austria, Hungary, Romania, Croatia, Slovakia, Poland, Ukraine, and parts of Italy.

## JAPAN

Japan declared war on Germany in 1914 and defeated German troops in China.

## AUSTRALIA AND NEW ZEALAND

Members of the British Empire, Australia and New Zealand followed Britain into war on August 4, 1914. The Australian and New Zealand Army Corps, known as ANZAC, formed in 1915 and served in the Middle East, on the western front, and in the Gallipoli Campaign for control of Constantinople (now Istanbul, Turkey).

Indian cavalry served on the western front and in other areas during the war.

Map labels:
UNITED KINGDOM · BELGIUM · FRANCE · ITALY · PORTUGAL · TUNISIA · MOROCCO · ALGERIA · LIBYA · FRENCH WEST AFRICA · TOGO · NIGERIA · PORT. GUINEA · SIERRA LEONE · LIBERIA · GOLD COAST · KAMERUN · FR. EQ. AFRICA · BELGIAN CONGO · ANGOLA · N. RHODESIA · GERMAN SOUTH-WEST AFRICA · BECHUANALAND · UNION OF SOUTH AFRICA · S. RHODESIA · MADAGASCAR · PORTUGUESE EAST AFRICA · GERMANY · AUSTRIA-HUNGARY · MONTENEGRO · SERBIA · ROMANIA · BULGARIA · GREECE · OTTOMAN EMPIRE · EGYPT · NAJD · OMAN · KUWAIT · ANGLO-EGYPTIAN SUDAN · ERITREA · FRENCH SOMALILAND · BRITISH SOMALILAND · ITALIAN SOMALILAND · UGANDA · BRITISH EAST AFRICA · GERMAN EAST AFRICA · NYASALAND · RUSSIA · CHINA · NEPAL · INDIA · SIAM · FRENCH INDOCHINA · MALAY STATES · JAPAN · TSINGTAO · PHILIPPINES · KAISER WILHELM'S LAND · PAPUA · AUSTRALIA · NEW ZEALAND

Legend:
- Allied nations
- Central powers
- Neutral nations

## FRONTLINE FACT  FOUR EMPIRES COLLAPSED AT THE END OF WWI.

# BIG BATTLES

## MISERY AND MAYHEM WERE THE ORDER OF THE DAY ON THE WORLD WAR I BATTLEFIELD. CAMPAIGNS, BATTLES, AND SKIRMISHES

were fought on land, at sea, and in the air. New tactics and weaponry such as tanks, big howitzer guns, and more accurate machine guns, grenades, and rifles, made this war more brutal and deadly than previous wars.

### BATTLE OF TANNENBERG
#### AUGUST 26–30, 1914

World War I had two fronts: the eastern front and the western front. The first big battle fought on the eastern front saw German soldiers crush Russian forces—almost destroying the Russian First and Second Armies. Nearly 250,000 Russian soldiers died, while Germany lost fewer than 20,000 men.

### BATTLE FOR GALLIPOLI
#### FEBRUARY 1915 TO JANUARY 1916

Gallipoli was considered one of the biggest failures for the Allies. The battle, also called the Dardanelles Campaign, took place in the Gallipoli Peninsula, which is part of modern-day Turkey. The Allies launched a sea and land offensive against the Ottoman Turks that lasted almost a year and claimed 46,000 lives. It was abandoned by the Allies and became a source of pride and sorrow for both the Turks who won and the ANZAC troops who lost.

### BATTLE OF VERDUN
#### FEBRUARY TO DECEMBER 1916

One of the deadliest battles in the history of war, the Battle of Verdun took place in and around the ancient fortified town of Verdun, France. This long and costly fight claimed an estimated 600,000 French and German lives. Another 750,000 were wounded. Exact totals were difficult to count as many bodies were lost in the slippery, quicksand-like mud created when pockmarked land became rain soaked.

## BATTLE OF JUTLAND
### MAY 31 TO JUNE 1, 1916

One of the largest naval actions in military history, the Battle of Jutland pitted the German Navy against the British Royal Navy in the North Sea near Jutland, Denmark. Both sides claimed victory despite heavy losses—14 battleships and cruisers for Britain and 11 for Germany. Germany used zeppelin airships for reconnaissance and bombing as well as U-boat submarines.

## THIRD BATTLE OF YPRES
### JULY TO NOVEMBER 1917

One of the muddiest and most difficult battles of the war took place on the western front at the village of Passchendaele, Belgium. Constant shelling and rainy weather turned the soil into thick, heavy mud that stopped tanks and clogged guns. Soldiers and horses waded through hip-deep muck—some even drowned in it. The Allies finally captured the village, but suffered heavy losses. Close to 300,000 Allied soldiers died.

**FRONTLINE FACT**   DREADNOUGHTS WERE BATTLESHIPS PROPELLED BY STEAM AND MOUNTED WITH BIG GUNS.

# AN ILLUSTRATED DIAGRAM

## IN THE TRENCHES

## THE GUNFIRE WAS CONSTANT AND DEADLY

### ON THE FRONT LINES. THE CERTAINTIES OF LIFE IN THE TRENCHES

were mud, fear, lice, and lousy food. In no other war were trenches used so extensively. Trench systems stretched from Belgium, through France, and into Switzerland. Soldiers learned to loathe their cold and cramped quarters, but the only thing worse was emerging from the earthen pits for an assault on no-man's-land.

### FRONTLINE TRENCH

This is where the real battle action happened. Guns fired and attacks launched from the front line.

**NO-MAN'S-LAND:** This was the land between the Allies' and the Central Powers' trench systems. It was a destruction zone, with huge craters made from the artillery fire, as well as barbed wire and dead bodies.

**SUPPORT TRENCH:** Men and supplies were kept safe in this second layer of trenches. They were used to support the soldiers on the front line. Reserve trenches, usually located behind support trenches, were used to give soldiers a break from fighting.

**COMMUNICATION TRENCH:** The trenches connected the reserve, support, and front line. Messages, supplies, and men moved through the system along these trenches.

**DUGOUT:** This was a small, sheltered room dug off from a trench.

**FRONTLINE FACT** RATS WERE A COMMON ENEMY OF ALL SOLDIERS IN WWI TRENCHES.

Soldiers stare at the enemy's trench across the battlefield and no-man's-land. The shattered trees in the background show how destructive the fighting was. The front lines destroyed forests, farmers' fields, and villages, and they permanently pockmarked the landscape.

# 2
# TOTAL WAR

# WAR ON LAND

German troops aim rifles on a trench wall.

## THE SCREAMING SOUND
### OF MORTAR SHELLS AND WHIZZING BULLETS

welcomed soldiers to the front lines of World War I. Horses and men trudged through thick mud while the battle lines mostly stood still. Bigger guns, newer killing machines, and heavy casualties made this war on land different from wars that had been fought before.

## ON THE FRONTS

Within months of World War I's outbreak, it became apparent the old battle styles would not work. Battle lines on the western front became fixed as trenches were built, and rushing to a battle line meant a death sentence. WWI became known as a war of attrition—a war where each side tried to wear the enemy down through continuous loss of life and equipment.

**FRONTLINE FACT** THOUSANDS OF WOMEN SERVED AS NURSES AT THE FRONT AND IN WAR HOSPITALS AT HOME.

## AT WHAT COST?

The human cost of the land battles during the Great War was staggering. On the first day of the Battle of the Somme in France in 1916, approximately 20,000 British soldiers were killed. After five months of fighting over six miles (9.6 km) of land, the total of dead, wounded, and missing for both sides numbered more than one million. Epic land battles exhausted the morale of the remaining troops and used millions of dollars in resources.

**Rats such as those captured here were a common sight in the muddy land trenches of the war.**

### THE BRITISH AND FRENCH LOST MORE THAN 600,000 HORSES BY THE END OF 1917.

The Battalion of Death was a Russian all-women battalion that served on the eastern front.

The Christmas truce was a brief moment of quiet on the battlefront.

## CHRISTMAS TRUCE

On Christmas Eve, 1914, an extraordinary trench truce happened. Both sides unofficially stopped fighting to celebrate the holiday, and soldiers climbed out of the trenches to exchange gifts of plum puddings and other treats. They even played soccer together in no-man's-land. The truce didn't last long, though, and soldiers were forced back to fighting.

The British passenger liner RMS *Lusitania* was sunk by German U-boats while on its way from New York to Liverpool.

# NAVAL STRENGTH

The German and British navies were the strongest in the world in 1914. Britain had more ships, but Germany had better technology. Here's how their fleets compared by the numbers:

**301** destroyers were commanded by the British.

**144** destroyers were commanded by the Germans.

**65** British submarines patrolled the seas.

**29** German U-boats were employed to sink ships.

**64** cruisers were in Britain's fleet.

**14** German dreadnought battleships sailed the oceans.

Propaganda posters used inspiring art and slogans to encourage men to join the navy during the war.

JOIN THE NAVY
THE SERVICE FOR FIGHTING MEN

—Babcock—

# WAR AT SEA

## MODERN NAVAL WARFARE
### EMERGED DURING WORLD WAR I, WITH THE FIRST
use of aircraft carriers and wide-scale use of submarines. Command of the sea enabled a country to send—or prevent the sending of—troops and supplies to the front, determining the fate of the war.

## THE SINKING OF THE *LUSITANIA*
Germany excelled at sinking merchant and supply ships—preventing them from reaching their destinations. And the German Navy sent out a warning that they would sink all ships that entered British waters. On May 7, 1915, a German U-boat sank the RMS *Lusitania*, a passenger ship traveling from New York City to Liverpool, England, carrying 1,959 passengers. The U-boat torpedoed the *Lusitania* off the coast of Ireland, killing all but 764 passengers within 20 minutes. Germany justified the sinking by saying the *Lusitania* may have been carrying some military supplies. This enraged the United States, which lost 128 citizens with the sinking, and was one reason that the U.S. joined the war.

## A SUBMARINE BY ANOTHER NAME
*Unterseeboots*, or "undersea boats" (U-boats) were German submarines that attacked any ship in the waters around Britain. Before 1915, the worldwide agreement was that submarines had to surface before they attacked another ship. This gave the passengers time to evacuate the ship before it was sunk. But this agreement was soon ignored during the war. The Germans attacked by complete surprise, sinking many Allied supply ships.

## DAZZLE ME
It's hard to hide a battleship in the open ocean. Most were painted gray to blend in with the water. But wakes and smoke made by the ships helped enemies identify the ships' locations. So, the British Royal Navy tried something different in 1917. They used "dazzle" camouflage, or bold stripes and bright colors, to baffle the enemy. The camouflage didn't hide a ship—it confused the enemy about where the ship's outline was, making the ship hard to attack.

**FRONTLINE FACT** IN 1916, GERMAN U-BOATS SANK NEARLY 500 SHIPS IN FOUR MONTHS.

# WAR IN THE AIR

## AIRPLANES WERE A RECENT

**INVENTION WHEN WORLD WAR I BROKE OUT. AS** battlefields moved to the skies, fighter planes dodged bullets and pilots known as "aces" showed their daring skills. This new age of in-air warfare paved the way for fighter squadrons and troops that fought in the air—the "air force."

## DOGFIGHTS IN THE AIR

A dogfight was an air-combat tactic first used with fighter planes in World War I. They were named after the intense, violent fights dogs sometimes get into. Pilots flying one-seater or two-seater open-cockpit airplanes dodged enemy airplanes in midair. Sometimes the fight was over when a plane was shot down. Or it could last until one of the planes ran out of fuel. Either way, the pilot usually went down with the plane.

## GIANT AIRSHIPS

Huge, slow, and also deadly, German zeppelin airships were used to observe from the air and as air-bombing machines during WWI. These giant airships were filled with hydrogen gas and they could carry heavy bombs, but they had a huge flaw—the gas could easily catch fire. German zeppelins carried out bombing raids on London, England, killing people and destroying buildings. By 1916, British defenses against zeppelin raids improved, and many were shot down.

## FLYING ACES

As battles by air increased, some fighter pilots stood out as "aces" for their air victories. Here are some of the brightest and most brilliant WWI fighter pilots.

**THE RED BARON:** Manfred von Richthofen, known as the Red Baron, was the best known WWI flying ace. A national hero in Germany, the Red Baron was a nobleman who, in his flashy red plane, shot down 80 Allied fighters. He was shot down in 1918 while pursuing an Allied fighter plane.

**BILLY BISHOP:** This Canadian fighter pilot first showed his skills in early 1917. He shot down 72 German planes by the time the war ended.

**RENÉ FONCK:** This French flyer was the best of the Allied aces. He shot down a total of 75 enemy planes.

**EDDIE RICKENBACKER:** A former race-car driver, this U.S. pilot was known for his speed and coolness. He was the top-scoring U.S. pilot, who shot down 26 enemy planes during the war.

**FRONTLINE FACT** MACHINE GUNS MOUNTED ON A PLANE FIRED THROUGH THE PLANE'S PROPELLERS.

## MAGNIFICENT FLYING MACHINES

The airplanes of WWI were flimsy and slow, made out of canvas and wooden frames. The open cockpit made flying cold and windy for pilots. Thin wires were used to brace the wings and tail, and top speeds were only 100 miles an hour (161 km/h).

**GOGGLES—** shielded the pilot's eyes from wind and debris

**LEATHER FLYING HELMETS—** protected the pilot's head from cold winds

**SCARF—** for warmth and ease of movement

**LEATHER COAT—** Leather is windproof and made flying in an open cockpit more comfortable.

**LEATHER GLOVES—** more durable and wind-proof than wool for keeping hands warm when flying

**PANTS AND PUTTEES—** Most pilots wore warm wool britches with puttees, or strips of cloth, wrapped around their calves.

**VON RICHTHOFEN**

**BISHOP**

**FONCK**

**RICKENBACKER**

# THE FIELD HOSPITAL

## MILLIONS OF WOUNDED AND DYING SOLDIERS WERE
### TREATED IN TRENCHES OR TRANSPORTED TO FIELD HOSPITALS. THESE HOSPITALS,
housed in the remains of bombed-out buildings or under tents, were crude but they saved many lives.

Nurses tend to the wounded in the frontline trenches before sending them to field hospitals.

### EXPLORER'S CORNER

It was very difficult to get wounded soldiers out of the front lines. Hospitals were a long way back and hard to reach. Enter the ambulance drivers, some of the many heroes of World War I. These daring young people—including teenagers, American volunteers such as novelist Ernest Hemingway, and many women—saved thousands of lives. Driving lightweight Ford Model T trucks and other vehicles, they bounced to the front over trenches and craters. They picked up wounded soldiers and drove them to hospitals.

### FROM BATTLEFIELD TO HOSPITAL

For wounded soldiers, stretcher bearers dodged corpses and bullets to treat minor wounds in the trenches. The more seriously injured were carried from the front lines to medical stations in the trenches or waiting ambulances. Field hospitals were crude tents staffed with doctors and nurses who treated everything from dysentery to amputations.

## TRENCH DISEASES

Soldiers had to fight another enemy while in the trenches—disease. With dead bodies, wet conditions, and vermin scurrying about, diseases such as typhoid, a deadly fever, spread quickly. Wounds and cuts had to be kept clean as there were no drugs to fight infections that could easily become deadly.

**Many soldiers were taught basic first aid so they could help their injured comrades.**

## TRENCH FOOT AND MOUTH

Many soldiers developed trench foot, a painful infection that could make their toes fall off and was caused by having constantly wet feet. To prevent it, soldiers had to rub their feet in whale oil, change their socks several times a day, and try to keep their feet dry. Dental care was the last thing soldiers thought about in the trenches. Bad or no brushing plus the stress of trench life led to trench mouth. It resulted in bleeding gums, loose teeth, and very bad breath.

**An ad for a trench disease treatment**

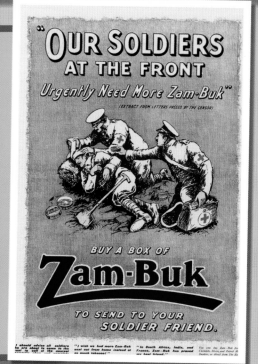

## SHELL SHOCK

Uncontrollable shaking, crippling paralysis, deafness, and blindness were just some of the many symptoms of a battlefield disorder called shell shock that was epidemic during World War I. A whopping 35,000 men unraveled with the condition during the Battle of the Somme. So many were affected that the British government set up convalescent hospitals and new treatments. Shell shock was caused by the constant fear and trauma of life on the battlefield and was the most common injury of the war. Today, the disorder is recognized as post-traumatic stress disorder and is treated as a legitimate health condition. But in WWI, men who suffered from shell shock and could not make themselves fight any longer were thought to be faking. Many were considered cowards and shot.

**Quiet activities such as gardening were part of shell shock treatment.**

**FRONTLINE FACT** MOBILE X-RAY MACHINES WERE USED IN WWI FIELD HOSPITALS.

# A PHOTO GALLERY

## IT TOOK A LOT

**OF PREPARATION TO** keep the troops fighting on the front lines. Supplies of food and ammunition had to be transported to the battle sites. Injured soldiers had to be transported out.

Officers eat a meal at a formal table with flowers, set up in a trench in France.

French troops and their war horses transport materials to the battle sites.

Italian troops fought in the Alps mountain range in northern Italy. The rough terrain meant troops used mountain dogs to carry supplies and rescue soldiers.

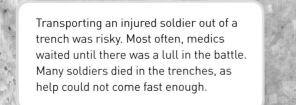

Transporting an injured soldier out of a trench was risky. Most often, medics waited until there was a lull in the battle. Many soldiers died in the trenches, as help could not come fast enough.

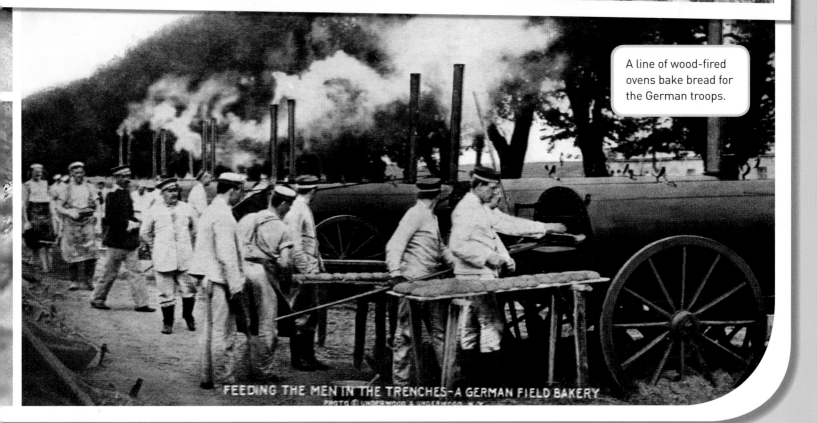

A line of wood-fired ovens bake bread for the German troops.

FEEDING THE MEN IN THE TRENCHES—A GERMAN FIELD BAKERY
PHOTO © UNDERWOOD & UNDERWOOD, N.Y.

# WAR FRONT AND HOME FRONT

Women played a crucial role in World War I as munitions workers in factories. It was difficult and dangerous work. Explosions and exposure to toxic chemicals killed 400 women workers in British factories during the war.

# WEAPONS AND TACTICS

*RAT-A-TAT-TAT! BOOM!* **WWI WEAPONS DELIVERED A DEADLY PUNCH. FROM RAPID-FIRE MACHINE GUNS TO BIG** artillery guns and tanks, the weaponry of this modern war made it the most advanced the world had seen.

## THE BIG GUNS

Massive, long-barreled howitzer guns made the battlefield a noisy place. Some of these heavy, long-range guns were transported by trains instead of horses, and were called railway guns. Railway guns were used on the western front and required specially constructed locomotives for transport. Another gun with a big size and reputation was Germany's Big Bertha, or *Dicke Bertha* in German. It was a heavy howitzer artillery gun with 16.5-inch (42-cm) barrel that shot shells that weighed 2,100 pounds (952 kg).

**FRONTLINE FACT** WWI-ERA MACHINE GUNS OFTEN OVERHEATED AND JAMMED.

## THROWING FIRE

Fire has always been a weapon of war. But the first mechanical flamethrowers were used as a shock weapon on the fronts of World War I. These portable weapons shot flames, using fuel oil, pressure from nitrogen, and a spark. The Germans first used flamethrowers at the Battle of Verdun in February 1916 and soon formed organized flamethrower troops, called *Flammenwerfer*. Flamethrowers were used to make troops fearful and clear them from trenches.

## TREACHEROUS TANKS

As the war at the front came to a stalemate, the Allies brought in a weapon that could crush barbed wire, cross trenches, and break through enemy lines. Tanks were moving killing machines first used on September 15, 1916, during the Battle of Flers-Courcelette on the western front. These "landships" weighed 28 tons (25 MT), had bigger guns with hundreds of shells, machine guns, and crews of up to eight men. Although they worked well on dry land, they could also get stuck in the mud.

## GAS ATTACK!

When the first greenish yellow cloud floated toward frontline troops at the Battle of Ypres in 1915, French and Algerian soldiers were caught by surprise. It didn't take long to figure out that this new weapon—chlorine gas—was a silent killer. The Allies had no protective gas masks for the first poison gas attacks. Soldiers ran wildly over the battlefield. They were blind—eyes stinging with tears—coughing and wheezing for air, and dying in droves. Soon after, gas attacks became all too common and masks became standard gear for soldiers. As the war progressed, other gases were used. So disgusted by the brutal effects of gassing, countries agreed to ban the use of poison gas after the war.

**Even dogs were outfitted with protective gas masks.**

## EXPLORER'S CORNER

New weapons were invented in the hopes that they would take control of the battlefield and end the war. But they never quite delivered what their inventors promised. Tanks broke down easily or tumbled upside down in giant craters. Airplanes were too fragile and slow, and couldn't carry enough bombs. Artillery and machine guns ruled the battlefields. Artillery killed more soldiers than any other weapon. The live artillery shells that still litter the battlefields today sometimes explode, killing or injuring people.

# BEHIND THE LINES

## BEHIND EVERY SOLDIER
### WHO WENT OFF TO WAR WAS A FAMILY WHO

supported the war effort at home. The war was a massive effort for both sides. Whole countries had to help, from the women left behind to the industries making armaments, food, and supplies. It was a total war and home fronts did what they could to support their troops.

**Making artillery shells and ammunition was dangerous work.**

## WOMEN IN WAR

They watched their brothers, husbands, and sons march off to war. In most countries, women couldn't enlist as soldiers, but they found other ways to help. Before the war, most women stayed at home. During the war, many worked in factories, building machine guns, bombs, and other war supplies. Women took over and did many of the jobs traditionally done by men, proving themselves just as skilled as men. They also served as nurses, cooks, and ambulance drivers behind the front lines. In Britain, the Women's Land Army provided labor on farms when the men were serving overseas.

**FRONTLINE FACT** MANY WOMEN WORKED IN FACTORIES MAKING MUNITIONS DURING THE WAR.

**WAR BONDS**

**FEED THE GUNS!**

BERT THOMAS

## WAR BONDS

From transporting troops, to keeping them fed and making weapons, war is expensive. To cover the costs of war, governments sold war bonds. These bonds were basically small loans to the country. People at home paid a certain amount for the bond. After a few years, they would get their money back with some interest added. Governments used war propaganda posters to urge citizens to invest in the war. Rallies with movie stars were held supporting the purchase of bonds as a patriotic duty. Governments raised billions through the sale of war bonds.

**ONE MILLION WOMEN WERE ADDED TO BRITAIN'S WORKFORCE FROM 1914 TO 1918.**

## BOY SOLDIERS

Hey, kid, want to join the army? Believe it or not, boys as young as 12 years old served in the armies of World War I. The official minimum age for signing up was 18, but lying about your age was common. A lot of kids were working to help support their families by the time they were 15, so the life of a soldier wasn't a huge leap. Some sources say up to 15 percent of recruits were under-age, especially near the end of the war, when armies were taking any volunteers they could get.

## ENEMY ALIENS

Being German in an Allied country during WWI was not a good thing. German immigrants became known as "enemy aliens" during the war. They were considered a threat, possibly even spies for the Germans. In some countries, people of German descent were imprisoned in camps. In Canada, 8,579 German-Canadians went to these camps. Australia forced 7,000 enemy aliens into camps. In the United States, 480,000 German aliens were registered as being threats.

A group of German-American children show their loyalty to the United States by parading around a neighborhood as soldiers.

# SECRETS AND SPIES

## ONE OF THE SECRETS TO WINNING A WAR WAS TO KEEP YOUR SECRETS SECRET. SPIES WERE LISTENING—ALWAYS. AND SPIES COULD make or break a war by giving valuable information about troop movements, battle strategy, and attack launch dates.

### FAMOUS SPIES

Some of the spies of WWI became famous for their daring and sometimes treacherous acts. Spying was dangerous—if caught, spies were shot.

**CARL HANS LODY:** This German spy served in the navy. He had been married to an American and spoke perfect English. He volunteered to become a spy and reported from Britain, but he wasn't a very good spy. Lody sent messages that were uncoded or in simple codes. The British Security Service intercepted his letters and Lody was arrested on October 2, 1914. He was executed on November 6, 1914.

**MARTHE RICHER:** This French female pilot became a double agent for the French and the Germans. She later lived in France and became well known for her spying efforts during the war.

**MATA HARI:** This Dutch dancer was shot by a French firing squad in 1917. Accused of being a double agent who was spying for both the French and the Germans, there was slim evidence that she actually did spy for Germany. Mata Hari mingled with the rich and famous, traveling across Europe. Her racy life made her an easy target for rumor and stories.

**Mata Hari was known for her exotic dancing costumes.**

### CODES AND CODE BREAKERS

A good way to trip up enemy "listeners" was to communicate in coded messages that were like puzzles. Codes used numbers to represent letters or foreign language words to represent letters of the alphabet. Codes were heavily used during WWI, and code breakers were the people who figured out the puzzle. For the Americans, one code worked really well—using the Native American Choctaw language. Some Choctaw soldiers became the Choctaw Code Talkers. Their messages stumped the Germans and helped the Allies win the battles of St. Étienne and Forest Ferme.

**Spies risked death by firing squad.**

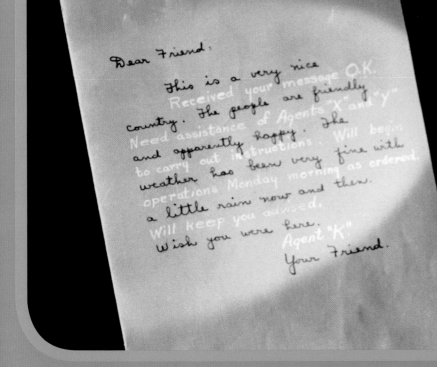

Dear Friend,

This is a very nice country. The people are friendly and apparently happy. The weather has been very fine with a little rain now and then. Wish you were here.

Your Friend.

Received your message O.K. Need assistance of Agents "X" and "Y" to carry out instructions. Will begin operations Monday morning as ordered. Will keep you advised.

Agent "K"

## SECRET SPY TRICKS

WWI spies used some interesting gadgets and tricks to get and send secret information. Here are a few of the best:

**INVISIBLE INK:** Different countries had different formulas for invisible ink. The Germans used crushed aspirin and water. Lemon juice and potassium also made good ink. Once used, it would dry to be invisible on the paper. When water or another liquid was pressed on the paper, the message would suddenly appear.

**SECRET TATTOOS:** Invisible messages were also painted on people's bodies. Spraying a liquid on the skin revealed the messages.

**ENGRAVED TOENAILS:** Some spies carved tiny messages on their toenails.

**HIDDEN CAMERAS:** Pigeons were used as spies. They carried messages and some had small cameras attached to their bodies for photos.

## SPY TREES?

Even trees couldn't be trusted in WWI! Both sides made special spy trees that were set up in no-man's-land. British artists chose a bombed-out tree stump on the front lines. They photographed and studied it, and then they sent sketches and photographs of the tree to a workshop. Artists created a copy of the tree using steel cylinders and bark. In the middle of the night, soldiers cut down the real tree and dug out its stump. Then they replaced it with the fake tree. The middle of the fake tree was hollow, allowing a soldier to climb inside and spy on or shoot at the enemy. Spies inside could see what enemies were doing in their trenches.

**FRONTLINE FACT** THE BRITISH USED 45 SPY TREES DURING THE WAR.

# ARMISTICE AND REMEMBRANCE

Leaders meet to sign the armistice agreement in Versailles, France, that ended the war.

## THE WAR ENDED NOT WITH
### A FINAL FRIGHTENING BATTLE, BUT WITH THE
signing of a deal between the Allies and Germany called the armistice agreement. The fighting stopped on November 11, 1918, at 11 a.m.

## MISERY, REVOLT, AND HUNGER

By the end of the war, millions of troops and civilians were dead. A large part of the French Army rebelled in 1917, refusing to fight. And in Russia, a revolution forced the tsar to give up his crown while the new government withdrew from war. By the time the armistice was signed, the world of old alliances had crumbled, and the German, Ottoman, and Austro-Hungarian Empires were no more. Food shortages in Europe and diseases such as typhus, spread by rat fleas, were killing people who had managed to survive the fighting.

Poppies are often used as a symbol of remembrance for those who died in WWI.

# TREATY OF VERSAILLES

The armistice brought the fighting to an end, but the Treaty of Versailles brought the war to an end. This peace treaty was signed on June 28, 1919, at the Versailles Palace, near Paris, France. The treaty established the League of Nations, an international group designed to settle disputes; ended the German Empire; and gave new (and smaller) boundaries to Germany. Germany was forced to accept responsibility for the war and pay reparations, or money to the countries it fought. The harsh repayments played a part in the development of the Second World War in 1939.

**Germany had to surrender weapons and territory and pay reparations under the Treaty of Versailles.**

# LEST WE FORGET

Whether it is called Armistice Day, Remembrance Day, or Veterans Day—every year on November 11, countries around the world remember the sacrifices made by those who served in war. Often, the remembrance includes ceremonies and a moment of silence at 11 a.m. to mark the ceasefire of 1918. In Australia and New Zealand, April 25 is Anzac Day, a national day of remembrance. April 25, 1915, was the day the ANZAC troops landed at Gallipoli.

# DIGGING UP THE WAR

Many frontline battles took place in farmers' fields and even today farmers still find remnants of the Great War while working the land. Some fields are grave sites, while others have unexploded grenades, gas canisters, and shells. These metal shells and grenades gradually work their way to the soil's surface. The farmers call this the "iron harvest."

# MARKING THE PLACE

Drive through the European countryside where the war took place and it would be hard to miss a World War I cemetery. Row upon row of white gravestones or crosses mark the resting place of millions of soldiers. Many countries have built monuments and memorials near the grave sites to honor those who had no known grave. One of the largest, the Canadian National Vimy Memorial, is a massive, soaring memorial on Vimy Ridge in France. It marks the battle that took place there and the men who died fighting.

**FRONTLINE FACT**  MANY UNEXPLODED SHELLS ARE FOUND EACH YEAR NEAR THE FORMER WWI FRONT LINES.

# FRONTLINE COMPARISONS

## WWI SOLDIER VS. MODERN SOLDIER

**SOME THINGS** **CHANGE IN WAR AND SOME** things stay the same. It's not so hard to imagine how soldiers lived and felt during the First World War when you compare these images.

## SAYING GOODBYE

Troops "shipped out" by train during World War I, whereas today's soldiers gather on base and are flown to sites of war.

# HAIRSTYLES

A haircut at the front lines usually meant a fellow soldier cutting with scissors. Electric clippers do the job today.

# COMBAT

Soldiers went "over the top" of the trenches, engaging in battle nearby—today's soldiers are more mobile.

# PLANES

WWI fighter planes were made from lightweight wood with open cockpits. Today's fighter jets have computers and glass cockpits and also carry missiles.

# 4
# WAR GAMES

During off-hours, soldiers enjoyed musical nights. Many popular songs, such as "Over There" and "It's a Long Way to Tipperary," were WWI hits that are still well known today.

# SUITS, BOOTS, AND SLANG

## SOLDIERS LIVED IN THEIR UNIFORMS.
### THEY WERE THEIR PROTECTION, THEIR IDENTITY, AND EVEN THEIR

pajamas. Through the cold winters and muddy conditions on the European fronts, soldiers wore their wool uniforms day and night. Here's a look at what WWI soldiers wore in the trenches. See if you can match parts of the uniform to their purpose.

**1. DRAB-COLORED FABRIC**

**2. GAITERS**

**3. SAM BROWNE BELT**

**4. HOBNAILED TRENCH BOOTS**

**5. SERVICE, OR CAMPAIGN HAT**

**6. PUTTEES**

**a.** This uniform part made it easy to carry a sword. It was first worn by the British and later the French, Americans, and Belgians. After 1918, the Germans wore it too. One-armed British officer Sam Browne invented it.

**b.** This uniform essential, worn by the doughboys and British Tommies, or regular soldiers, kept feet warm, but water could still seep in and cause trench foot. Hobnails were nailed into the soles to give soldiers better traction in the trenches.

**c.** Blending in to their surroundings helped keep soldiers alive. The Germans wore gray-green uniforms, the French wore blue, and the British and U.S. troops wore khaki uniform tunic and trousers or breeches. Up until WWI, many military uniforms were brightly colored. But new weapons used in this war could hit targets at 500 yards (457 m) or more away, making bright colors deadly.

**d.** These long strips of cloth wound around soldiers' legs from ankle to knee for protection and support.

**e.** A cotton or canvas protective covering for boots and lower breeches.

**f.** This head gear had colored cord that showed which branch of service the soldier served in. They were later replaced by wool caps that were easier to store.

**FRONTLINE FACT**   TEN PERCENT OF NEW ZEALAND'S POPULATION OF ONE MILLION FOUGHT IN WWI.

ANSWERS:
1.c; 2.e; 3.a; 4.b; 5.f; 6.d

# FRONTLINE SLANG

"That doughboy there sure is a skateboard ace and he's in A-1 shape. While the rest of us sit around chatting, he pulls a maneuver that would have had me in a tailspin!" Some of the words we use every day have their roots in World War I soldier slang. Soldiers came up with these informal words to describe what they saw, heard, and felt. Here's some WWI slang from the front lines:

**A-1:** In top form

**ACE:** An excellent performer or top pilot

**BRASS HAT:** A high-ranking officer

**CHAT:** Lice

**CHATTING:** Removing lice

**DIGGING-IN:** To establish a position; digging into the trenches

**DOUGHBOY:** A U.S. soldier

**DUD:** Something that failed

**FED UP:** To be weary

**HUSH-HUSH:** Top secret operation

**IN A TAILSPIN:** Out of control

**LANDOWNER:** To be dead and buried

**LOUSY:** Infested with lice

**NO-MAN'S-LAND:** The destroyed area between the opposing lines of the war

**REST CAMP:** A cemetery

**SHELL SHOCK:** To suffer from trauma and stress because of the constant bombing and gunfire

**TOMMY:** A British soldier

**TRENCH COAT:** A waterproof coat with a belt; worn in the trenches

**Z-HOUR:** The time an attack was to start

These soldiers are "chatting away," or picking lice off their clothing.

# HEADS UP!

Headgear is important to a soldier. On the battlefield, headgear protects the soldier's head from shell fragments. Off the battlefield, caps of all kinds were worn.

**PITH HELMET:** A light helmet made of cork wood, called pith. It was worn by British troops fighting in the Middle East and Africa.

**PICKELHAUBE (OR POINTE BONNET):** This German helmet had a central spike on its top.

**KEPI:** This flat-topped circular cap was worn by French troops.

# EXPLORER'S CORNER

War was not all misery for the soldiers. On the march, in the trenches, and under fire they formed friendships that would last all their lives. They played pranks, games, and sports, and switched from their uniforms to costumes for comedic plays. Groups of soldiers sang popular songs in the trenches or while they marched. The lucky ones got to enjoy concerts or take short vacations in Paris. Soldier Bruce Bairnsfather became popular for the cartoons he drew poking fun at life in the trenches. Many soldiers said that a sense of humor was necessary for survival.

# WAR HEROES

## THEY RISKED LIFE AND LIMB FOR THEIR COMRADES
### AND THEIR COUNTRIES. WWI WAS FILLED WITH DARING HEROES. SOME DISAPPEARED
on the battlefields, but others were known around the world.

### THE HARLEM HELLFIGHTERS

The first African-American unit to fight in WWI was one of the toughest of all the troops. Their nickname, "Harlem Hellfighters," wasn't given to them for nothing. They were fierce soldiers on the battlefield who served for six months on the front lines. Their service earned them France's highest medal of honor—the Croix de Guerre. The Harlem Hellfighters was the first U.S. unit to ever receive this honor.

### THE HELLO GIRLS

Telephone operators kept the communication lines open during the war, and this group of U.S. women "switchboard soldiers" kept the lines open even during major attacks. The "Hello Girls" connected the men on the front lines with commanders at their headquarters, speaking both English and French, so they could translate messages from French generals to U.S. commanders.

**FRONTLINE FACT** SIXTY-FOUR VICTORIA CROSS MEDALS WERE AWARDED TO SOLDIERS DURING WWI.

## EXTRAORDINARY SERGEANT YORK

He was one of the most decorated U.S. heroes. Alvin "Sergeant" York showed his strength and bravery during the Meuse-Argonne Offensive and forever became a symbol of patriotic soldiering. Firing at a nest of German machine guns, he didn't give up and kept shooting until the Germans surrendered. Sergeant York then took 132 enemy prisoners. For his actions that day, York was awarded the Congressional Medal of Honor.

**SERGEANT ALVIN YORK**

## CRACK SHOT, DARING ACE

William George "Will" Barker was a farm boy from Manitoba, Canada, whose shooting and flying skills helped make him Canada's most decorated soldier. As a flying ace, Barker earned 12 awards for valor, including the Victoria Cross, three military crosses, and a French Croix de Guerre. His Victoria Cross was awarded for a series of daring dogfights on October 27, 1918, when he was severely wounded in his legs and elbow and still shot down several German aircraft. He passed out while flying but recovered before crash landing and being pulled from the wreckage.

**WILLIAM BARKER**

## FRIEND TO SOLDIERS

This British nurse did all that she could to help injured soldiers—both Allied and German. When the town she was stationed in was taken over by Germans, she stayed at her post. The Germans didn't want her to help the Allies, though. In August 1915, they arrested her for helping 200 Allied prisoners escape to Holland. After admitting that she did help the prisoners, she was sentenced to death. A German firing squad executed her on October 12, 1915. Her death outraged the British, and the Allies had even more support than before.

**EDITH CAVELL**

## IT'S AN HONOR!

Medals show just how much a country appreciates a soldier's service. Medals were given out for service and for specific battles. Some medals honored extreme courage or valor. Here are some of the top honors given during World War I.

### VICTORIA CROSS:

The highest award for gallantry for a British and British Empire serviceman. It is awarded for acts of extreme bravery.

### DISTINGUISHED SERVICE CROSS AND MEDAL OF HONOR:

These U.S. medals are the top two given to brave soldiers.

### IRON CROSS:

Germans received this medal for their distinguished service in the military.

### LÉGION D'HONNEUR AND CROIX DE GUERRE:

These French medals are the highest awards given to soldiers and civilians who served in war.

# AMAZING ANIMALS OF THE WAR

## THEY BARKED, CHIRPED,
### AND NEIGHED THEIR WAY THROUGH THE WAR.

The animal heroes of World War I helped in ways that might not be well remembered. But without them, the war would have been a lot more difficult than it already was.

### WAR HORSES— BEASTS OF BURDEN

An estimated eight million horses died on the front lines of WWI. With roads destroyed, horses pulled artillery and supplies through scarred landscapes near the front lines, often sinking deep into slippery mud. They carried infantry troops and sometimes were equipped with their own gas masks.

### FLYING SPIES

Spies of the skies—carrier pigeons—delivered messages and took secret photos. Many were used, but Cher Ami was the most famous. He flew for the U.S. Army Signal Corps and delivered 12 messages. Sadly, he was struck by an enemy's bullet and died in 1919.

**FRONTLINE FACT** GLOWWORMS ARE INSECT LARVAE WHOSE GLOW PROVIDED READING LIGHT TO SOLDIERS.

It's an obedient dog that will jump over barbed wire! Wolf the Alsatian dog did so every day on his way to deliver messages to troop commanders in the trenches of the western front.

# MEET SERGEANT STUBBY

The most famous dog of WWI was destined to be a star. Sergeant Stubby ended up on the battlefields and earned more war medals than his owner. This Boston terrier was smuggled to the front lines in France by U.S. Pvt. J. Robert Conroy. Stubby stayed there with the 102nd battalion. He warned the soldiers of gas attacks and found wounded soldiers on patrol. This brave dog also attacked a German spy! He was in 17 battles during the war and survived several wounds. He returned to the United States a hero.

# ANIMAL SOLDIERS

How did animals help on the front lines? See if you can match the animal with its war task.

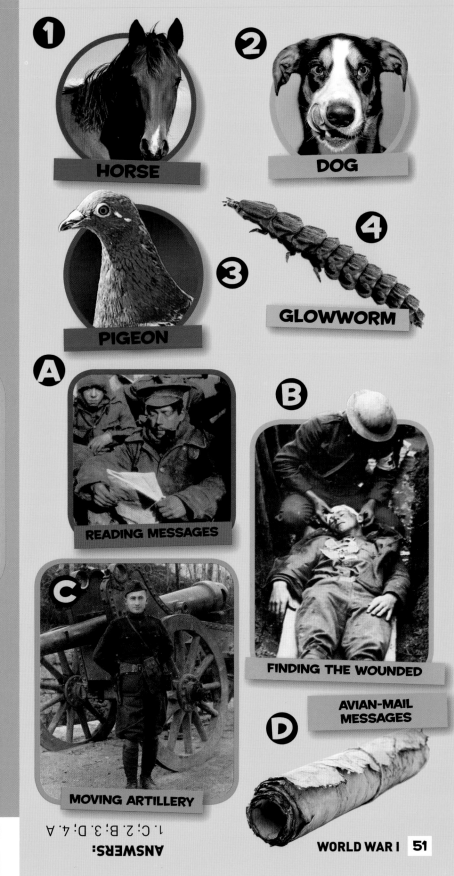

**1** HORSE

**2** DOG

**3** PIGEON

**4** GLOWWORM

**A** READING MESSAGES

**B** FINDING THE WOUNDED

**C** MOVING ARTILLERY

**D** AVIAN-MAIL MESSAGES

ANSWERS: 1.C; 2.B; 3.D; 4.A

WORLD WAR I **51**

# MYTH OR FACT?

## DID THAT REALLY HAPPEN
**IN WORLD WAR I? CAN YOU GUESS WHICH WWI** stories are fact and which are fiction?

**A** U.S. PRESIDENT WOODROW WILSON'S CAMPAIGN SLOGAN WAS "WE WILL WIN THE WAR!"

**B** TRENCH RATS GREW TO THE SIZE OF CATS.

**C** HAMBURGERS WERE RENAMED "SALISBURY STEAKS" DURING THE WAR.

**D** A CANADIAN SURGEON BROUGHT A BEAVER TO EUROPE WHEN HE WENT TO SERVE IN THE WAR AND IT BECAME HIS TROOP'S MASCOT.

**E** SOLDIERS SOMETIMES PEED ON HANDKERCHIEFS TO MAKE HOMEMADE GAS MASKS.

**A. FICTION** Wilson's real slogan was "He kept us out of war." Shortly after taking office, though, he declared war on Germany.

CANADIAN DOCTOR CLUNY MACPHERSON INVENTED THE CHEMICAL WEAPON GAS MASK USING A CANVAS HOOD, EYEPIECES, AND A BREATHING TUBE.

**B. FACT** Rats in the trenches had lots of food to eat. They scrounged from the empty cans left by soldiers. They also ate the corpses of soldiers who had fallen on the battlefield. Rats grew huge and were a constant bother to the soldiers.

**FRONTLINE FACT** A STATUE OF WINNIE THE BEAR STANDS IN A PARK IN WINNIPEG, MANITOBA, CANADA.

**HAMBURGER**

**C. FACT** The name "hamburgers" came from the name of the German town of Hamburg. Americans didn't want anything to do with Germany, so they renamed this popular sandwich. Sauerkraut was renamed "liberty cabbage."

**SAUERKRAUT**

**D. FICTION** The soldier, Lt. Harry Colebourn of the Fort Garry Horse regiment brought a black bear cub with him. The bear was named Winnie for Lieutenant Colebourn's hometown of Winnipeg, Manitoba, Canada. When the regiment went to the front, Winnie stayed at the London Zoo. She became the inspiration for the famous children's stories of Winnie-the-Pooh because the author's son loved visiting the bear.

**E. FACT** Before soldiers were given gas masks, they had nothing to protect their lungs from gas attacks. Urine- or water-soaked cloth or pads became makeshift gas masks.

## BEHIND THE SHOT WITH EDWARD G. LENGEL

# A FEW YEARS AGO I TOURED A BATTLEFIELD
## NEAR VERDUN, FRANCE, WITH A GROUP OF PEOPLE THAT INCLUDED

my 12-year-old son. On this particular spot, American and German soldiers had fought for possession of a place called Molleville Farm. In the woods near the farm, we found trenches and pits where the soldiers put their machine guns. Nearby were piles of old wine bottles. We even discovered an old spoon from which some soldier had probably slurped his soup before the battle began.

As we continued through the woods, we discovered four large bunkers. These were like small buildings made of concrete and sunk partly underground. The Germans had built these to keep their soldiers safe from the American guns. When the Germans retreated, some Americans entered the bunkers to shelter from German artillery. It was still possible to enter these bunkers and walk through their dark halls that dripped with water. I imagined what it was like for the men who lived there—perhaps telling jokes to their friends even as they wondered whether they would survive the war to see their families and loved ones again.

At least one of those soldiers didn't make it. Leaving the bunker, my son helped to discover the remains of a soldier lying among the wet leaves. We will never know if the soldier was American or German. But there, almost 100 years after the war ended, the group of us gathered around the remains to pay our respects. Some of us even shed tears. As we left, we arranged for the remains to be buried properly in a beautiful French memorial at Verdun.

World War I seems like an awfully long time ago. But in that wet little forest near Verdun, bowing our heads at an unmarked grave, we knew that the men and women who experienced that war were people just like us. Just as we do, they laughed and cried, loved and suffered, lived and dreamed. Fighting on those battlefields, they thought that they were fighting "the war to end all wars" so that future generations—people like you and me—could live in peace. It would have consoled them to know that we, their children and grandchildren, would keep their memory alive in our hearts.

*They shall grow not old, as we that are left grow old:*
*Age shall not weary them, nor the years condemn.*
*At the going down of the sun and in the morning,*
*We will remember them.*

—"For the Fallen," by Laurence Binyon

War memorials sometimes list the names of the dead and are places where people leave wreaths and poppies to remember the sacrifices of those who fought.

The tangled barbed wire piled near a stark war memorial on Butte de Vauquois, a hill near Verdun, Varenne-en-Argonne, France, shows us World War I may be over, but it has not been forgotten. The landscape where noisy and frightening battles were fought 100 years ago still bears the scars of war.

# AFTERWORD

## THE LEGACY OF WORLD WAR I

### WARS ARE BRUTAL—IT'S A FACT—AND WWI WAS ESPECIALLY BRUTAL.

Millions of people, soldiers and civilians, were killed in the battles that took place over four years. Millions more died after the war from hunger and disease. An entire generation was lost—people who could have made their world a better place, but never got the chance. Those who survived were forever scarred by what they saw and did during the war. WWI not only cost lives, but it destroyed cities, towns, and countryside and left the environment a scorched ruin. It also cost countries and their militaries millions of dollars.

As fighting broke out, the Great War was called "the war to end all wars," but it quickly became a slaughter. The peace treaty that ended the war set harsh penalties against Germany, leaving its people and government feeling bitter and angry toward the Allies. It laid the foundation for future conflicts and another great war—World War II—that came roughly 20 years later.

But the war also destroyed or weakened the massive empires that had ruled the world, often harshly, for several centuries. In their place new countries and a new world order emerged, with the United States and a new, communist Russia (later the U.S.S.R.) leading the way. The aftermath of WWI gave rise to the League of Nations, the first international organization that attempted to keep world peace. It was the forerunner to the United Nations.

The world changed dramatically from 1914 to 1918. This period marked the beginning of a modern age where technology and social ideas advanced quickly. At the start of the war, troops were fighting using battle tactics that were centuries old. By the end, new weapons and even new branches of the military (air forces) were in place. Women, fully half the population, were in most countries not full citizens during the war, but just a few years later many gained the right to vote.

Although the veterans of the Great War are gone, each year we remember the sacrifices they made through Veterans Day and Remembrance Day services. Their acts truly changed the world.

Even as old men, these World War I veterans attending a remembrance service recalled the pain and loss as if it were yesterday.

Canadian soldier and field surgeon John McCrae wrote the poem "In Flanders Fields" after the Second Battle of Ypres in Belgium in 1915. It mentions the red poppies that grew on the graves of the war dead. The poem was published in a magazine and has since become a commonly recited remembrance poem in Canadian schools. It was the inspiration for the poppy campaign in the U.S., Canada, and other nations, where people buy and wear poppies to support disabled veterans. McCrae died in 1918.

## In Flanders Fields

*In Flanders fields the poppies blow
Between the crosses, row on row,
That mark our place; and in the sky
The larks, still bravely singing, fly
Scarce heard amid the guns below.*

*We are the Dead. Short days ago
We lived, felt dawn, saw sunset glow,
Loved, and were loved, and now we lie
In Flanders fields.*

*Take up our quarrel with the foe;
To you from failing hands we throw
The torch; be yours to hold it high.
If ye break faith with us who die,
We shall not sleep, though poppies grow
In Flanders fields.*

—John McCrae

Politicians from New Zealand, Turkey, and Australia mark the anniversary of the Battle of Gallipoli at a war memorial in Gallipoli, Turkey. April 25 is Anzac Day in Australia and New Zealand. It is a day of national remembrance where people attend dawn services and veterans parades.

# THEY KEPT THE SEA LANES OPEN

Some war art, like this illustration from a war bonds poster, was intended to inspire patriotism. Merchant ships, or the merchant marine, transported supplies across the Atlantic. Many merchant ships were sunk during the war.

# AN INTERACTIVE GLOSSARY

## FIGHTING WORDS

Mascots, such as these naval dogs, provided companionship and company to soldiers and sailors who went off to war.

# ACE YOUR WWI VOCABULARY!

## ARE YOU FIGHTING FIT FOR WORDS AND MEANINGS? USE THE GLOSSARY TO

learn what each word means and visit the page numbers listed to see the word used in context. Then test your WWI knowledge!

## 1. Armistice
A temporary promise to stop fighting a war
[PAGES 11, 40–41]

**At what time did the WWI armistice that ended the fighting take effect?**
a. 1 a.m.
b. noon
c. 11 a.m.
d. midnight

## 2. Artillery
Large and powerful guns used on land
[PAGES 7, 14, 19, 34–35, 36, 50, 54]

**What was the name of one of Germany's biggest artillery weapons?**
a. Large Marge
b. Big Bertha
c. Über Flammen
d. Big Ben

## 3. Assassination
The killing of an important or well-known person such as a politician or monarch
[PAGE 10]

**Whose assassination sparked the fighting in WWI?**
a. Archduke Franz Ferdinand
b. The Red Baron
c. Tzar Nicholas II
d. Prince Vladimir Paley

## 4. Campaign
A series of military actions done for a certain goal, confined to a specific area, or involving a certain type of fighting
[PAGES 15, 16, 46]

**What city did the Allies hope to win control over by fighting the Gallipoli Campaign?**
a. Berlin
b. Budapest
c. Hong Kong
d. Constantinople

## 5. Colony
A country or area that has been settled by another country and is controlled by that country
[PAGES 11, 13, 15]

**Which country was a British colony?**
a. Germany
b. Canada
c. France
d. Turkey

## 6. Dogfight
Combat in the air between military aircraft
[PAGES 26, 49]

**Which Canadian pilot shot down 72 German planes in dogfights during WWI?**
a. Arthur Whealey
b. The Red Baron
c. Billy Bishop
d. George Thomson

## 7. Draft
A required or compulsory service in the military during a time of war
[PAGE 13]

**How many American men were drafted into WWI?**
a. 2.8 million
b. 7 million
c. 600,000
d. 24 million

## 8. Reconnaissance
Military observation of an area to find an enemy or plan a battle strategy
[PAGE 17, 26]

**In which battle were zeppelins used for reconnaissance?**
a. Battle of Tannenberg
b. Battle of Verdun
c. Third Battle of Ypres
d. Battle of Jutland

## 9. Recruitment
The action of enlisting people to join the military
[PAGES 12, 14, 24, 37]

**How did the U.S. government try to recruit men into the army during WWI?**
a. Advertising on posters
b. Through television commercials
c. By giving away guns
d. Through concerts

## 10. Shell Shock
A disorder experienced by soldiers that is caused by the constant fear, trauma, and stress of warfare
[PAGES 29, 47]

**How many men were believed to have suffered from shell shock after fighting in the Battle of the Somme?**
a. 1,500
b. 14,000
c. 27,000
d. 35,000

## 11. Treaty
A formal agreement between governments and people or countries
[PAGES 41, 56]

**Which treaty brought WWI to an end?**
a. Treaty of Versailles
b. Treaty of Gallipoli
c. Treaty of the Croix de Guerre
d. Treaty of Berlin

## 12. Truce
An agreement between troops to stop fighting for a certain period of time
[PAGE 23]

**Over what holiday did a WWI truce occur?**
a. Easter
b. Christmas
c. Passover
d. Thanksgiving

**ANSWERS:**
1. c; 2. b; 3. a; 4. d; 5. b; 6. c; 7. a; 8. d; 9. a; 10. d; 11. a; 12. b

# FIND OUT MORE

Want to dig up great facts about the Great War? Try these resources to learn more.

## WWI GAMES AND VIDEOS

**Causes of World War I**
Visit www.bbc.co.uk/schools/gcsebitesize/history/mwh/ir1/causes_war1act.shtml to watch a fun presentation about the causes of World War I.

**Trench Warfare**
Visit www.bbc.co.uk/schools/worldwarone/hq/trenchwarfare.shtml to play a game about trench warfare during WWI.

*War Horse*
This movie follows a horse through the battlefields and trenches of WWI.

**WWI Pilot Training**
Visit www.airspacemag.com/history-of-flight/how-they-trained-44672147 to watch a video showing WWI pilot training in San Antonio, Texas.

## WEBSITES

**Kids: Ask your parents for permission to search online.**

**www.bbc.co.uk/schools/worldwarone**
World War One is a BBC website for kids that has letters from the war, WWI poetry, games, and a time line to explore.

**www.learnnc.org/lp/editions/ww1posters**
World War I Propaganda Posters is a site of the University of North Carolina. Click through a gallery of posters showing U.S. WWI propaganda.

## PLACES TO VISIT

**Museum of the Great War**
Peronne, France

**National World War I Museum**
Kansas City, MO, U.S.A.

## WWI BOOKS

*Everything Battles*
By John Perritano and James Spears
National Geographic Kids, 2013
Read about the action on the battlefield and learn everything you ever wanted to know about battles.

*Living Through World War I*
By Nicola Barber
Raintree, 2013
This books shows what it was like for the people who lived through World War I.

*Stubby the War Dog: The True Story of World War I's Bravest Dog*
By Ann Bausum
National Geographic Kids, 2014
This book tells the story of Sergeant Stubby, the most famous dog of World War I.

**BOLDFACE INDICATES ILLUSTRATIONS.**

**Published by the National Geographic Society**

Gary E. Knell, *President and Chief Executive Officer*

John M. Fahey, *Chairman of the Board*

Declan Moore, *Executive Vice President; President, Publishing and Travel*

Melina Gerosa Bellows, *Publisher and Chief Creative Officer, Books, Kids, and Family*

**Prepared by the Book Division**

Hector Sierra, *Senior Vice President and General Manager*

Nancy Laties Feresten, *Senior Vice President, Kids Publishing and Media*

Jennifer Emmett, *Vice President, Editorial Director, Kids Books*

Eva Absher-Schantz, *Design Director, Kids Publishing and Media*

Jay Sumner, *Director of Photography, Kids Publishing*

R. Gary Colbert, *Production Director*

Jennifer A. Thornton, *Director of Managing Editorial*

**NG Staff for This Book**

Shelby Alinsky, *Project Editor*

James Hiscott, Jr., *Art Director*

Lori Epstein, *Senior Photo Editor*

Margaret Leist, *Photo Assistant*

Callie Broaddus, *Design Production Assistant*

Carl Mehler, *Director of Maps*

David B. Miller, Martin S. Walz, *Map Research and Production*

Grace Hill, *Associate Managing Editor*

Joan Gossett, *Production Editor*

Lewis R. Bassford, *Production Manager*

Susan Borke, *Legal and Business Affairs*

**Production Services**

Phillip L. Schlosser, *Senior Vice President*

Chris Brown, *Vice President, NG Book Manufacturing*

George Bounelis, *Senior Production Manager*

Nicole Elliott, *Director of Production*

Rachel Faulise, Robert L. Barr, *Managers*

**Editorial, Design, and Production by Plan B Book Packagers**

10-1-14 OCLC

### Captions

Cover: Soldiers defend their trench while under shellfire on the western front of World War I

Back cover: World War I was fought using new technology, tactics, and weapons such as trench warfare and big guns on land and U-boats and convoys at sea.

Page 1: Airplanes were new to war. Dogfights were airplane battles that took place in the air.

Page 2–3: In the trenches, painted in 1917 by British war artist C.R.W. Nevinson. War artists were sent to paint scenes of the war.

The National Geographic Society is one of the world's largest nonprofit scientific and educational organizations. Founded in 1888 to "increase and diffuse geographic knowledge," the Society works to inspire people to care about the planet. National Geographic reflects the world through its magazines, television programs, films, music and radio, books, DVDs, maps, exhibitions, live events, school publishing programs, interactive media, and merchandise. *National Geographic* magazine, the Society's official journal, published in English and 38 local-language editions, is read by more than 60 million people each month. The National Geographic Channel reaches 320 million households in 38 languages in 171 countries. National Geographic Digital Media receives more than 25 million visitors a month. National Geographic has funded more than 10,000 scientific research, conservation, and exploration projects and supports an education program promoting geographic literacy.

For more information, please visit nationalgeographic.com, call 1-800-NGS LINE (647-5463), or write to the following address:
National Geographic Society
1145 17th Street N.W.
Washington, D.C. 20036-4688 U.S.A.

Visit us online at nationalgeographic.com/books

For librarians and teachers: ngchildrensbooks.org

More for kids from National Geographic:
kids.nationalgeographic.com

For information about special discounts for bulk purchases, please contact National Geographic Books Special Sales: ngspecsales@ngs.org

For rights or permissions inquiries, please contact National Geographic Books Subsidiary Rights: ngbookrights@ngs.org

**National Geographic supports K–12 educators with ELA Common Core Resources. Visit natgeoed.org/commoncore for more information.**

Paperback ISBN: 978-1-4263-1715-6
Reinforced library binding ISBN: 978-1-4263-1716-3

Printed in Hong Kong
14/THK/1